THE DEMOCRATS'
FORGOTTEN PEOPLE

THE DEMOCRATS'
FORGOTTEN PEOPLE

How the Trump Base Can Find a Home in the Democratic Party

Arthur Lieber

Columbus, Ohio

The Democrats' Forgotten People:
How the Trump Base Can Find a Home in the Democratic Party

Published by Gatekeeper Press
2167 Stringtown Rd, Suite 109
Columbus, OH 43123-2989
www.GatekeeperPress.com

Copyright © 2020 by Arthur Lieber

All rights reserved. Neither this book, nor any parts within it may be sold or reproduced in any form or by any electronic or mechanical means, including information storage and retrieval systems without permission in writing from the author. The only exception is by a reviewer, who may quote short excerpts in a review.

The editorial work for this book is entirely the product of the author. Gatekeeper Press did not participate in and is not responsible for any aspect of this element.

ISBN (paperback): 9781662904325
eISBN: 9781662904332

TABLE OF CONTENTS

Introduction vii

Chapter 1 – Overlooked by the Democratic Party 1

Chapter 2 – Reaching Out to the Forgotten People 9

Chapter 3 – Connecting Schools to the Common Good 37

Chapter 4 – Democratizing How Government Works 41

What We Can Do Now 61

Acknowledgments 63

INTRODUCTION

THE IDEA FOR THIS book was hatched less than 100 days prior to Election Day 2020. I was watching an effective advocate for a key identity group in the Democratic party. She was urging fellow panelists and the viewing audience to not forget her group, that they would be key to Joe Biden and his then-to-be-announced running mate secure the White House.

I couldn't disagree with her. I quickly downloaded her book explaining her advocacy. In my mind, it gave new meaning to the word *redundancy*. She posited arguments I had heard repeatedly from hundreds, perhaps thousands, of well-intentioned people. She thought we needed to be reminded of the importance of African Americans to the Democratic party, but it might as well have been Hispanics, recent immigrants, Native Americans, members of the LGBTQ community, young voters, senior citizens, or people without photo IDs who thought that they couldn't vote without one.

This was all well and good. Each of these interest groups had a history of being overlooked and were justified in fearing it could happen again, and again. It was important they defend themselves.

When I think of hardships to be overcome, my mind immediately races to poverty. If I had a Rolodex on poverty, I would frequently be pulling out cards from rural Alabama or the west side of Chicago or the barrios of Los Angeles. But I would also be looking at Harlan County, Kentucky, McDowell County in West Virginia, and Shannon County in Missouri.

What do those last three counties have in common? Two things of relevance here: they are overwhelmingly white, and for years they have consistently voted Republican.

The main thesis in this book is driven by two points related to the people in these counties. One, the Democratic party historically has and presently is much more responsive than the GOP to crafting policies to successfully deal with poverty. Two, the current Democratic party makes virtually no attempt to woo the kind of voters who live in these counties.

The poor white people of these counties are as much an identity group as African Americans or Hispanics. But they are forgotten. While it makes sense to "take" from other whites who are very wealthy in order to bring more equity to all the people in the country, it makes no sense to view poor white people as a basket of deplorables.

Addressing poverty must be a unifying principle of the Democratic party. John F. Kennedy said that a rising tide lifts all ships. If you lift people out of poverty, you will advance the economic well-being of those in the middle class and even those in the upper class.

When you lift people out of poverty, you will benefit people of all ethnicities. But if you leave a particular group behind, and the Democrats have been doing just that for the past 50 years, then you fragment the poverty coalition and weaken all ethnic groups within it. This book is a call to the Democratic party to not forget the millions of poor white people in the country who listen to hate and fear because the Democrats do not offer hope. This is a call for that hope.

Chapter 1

OVERLOOKED BY THE DEMOCRATIC PARTY

DEMOCRATS AND PROGRESSIVES ARE feeling pretty good about this upcoming election in November 2020. Frankly, I'm quite scared about this particular election and future ones as well.

What frightens me is that while Democrats try to include virtually every minority or aggrieved party in America's body politic, they are forgetting a group that has grievances as legitimate as all but a few other groups. I'm talking about the Trump base, largely white blue-collar workers (or nonworkers) who are struggling to make a living. These are Americans who are largely overlooked by the Democratic elite. They are the 2020 version of Archie and Edith Bunker. They are viewed with disdain by just about all segments of the current Democratic Party.

The odd thing is that blue-collar whites used to be the core of the Democratic constituency. Franklin D. Roosevelt's New Deal was designed to help people who were unemployed or underemployed find new ways of securing livable wages and job security. Granted, his primary focus was on white males, but that is the group that now wants little or nothing to do with the Democratic Party. Instead, they favor Donald Trump, who preys upon their worst instincts and further damages their economic well-being.

We might best call this group Forgotten Americans. It's a non-pejorative term and accurately describes their relationship with the elites of the Democratic Party. There is something unique about this group that is decidedly different from all other aggrieved groups. There are no leaders in the group, or perhaps more accurately, there are no leaders who advocate hope rather than fear. Forgotten Americans do have pseudo-leaders who tend to be purveyors of hate, conspiracy, and resentment. These charlatans are often rogue members of the clergy, right-wing talk radio personas, and Tea Party-type politicians.

Consider this in comparison to three other groups in America who have historically had their rights suppressed: African Americans, Hispanics, and women. Each has always had strong leadership as they fought for their justified civil rights.

1. African American leadership promoting hope, equal rights, and economic equality (since 1960—a partial list):
   - Ralph Abernathy
   - Muhammad Ali

- Stokely Carmichael (Kwame Ture)
- Elijah Cummings
- Marian Wright Edelman
- James Farmer
- Jesse Jackson
- Dr. Martin Luther King Jr.
- John Lewis
- Thurgood Marshall
- Al Sharpton
- Malcolm X

2. The Hispanic movement has had the following leaders:
   - Julian and Joaquin Castro
   - César Chavez
   - Henry Cisneros
   - Roberto Clemente
   - Jose Villar Diaz
   - Michelle Lujan Grisham
   - Lina Hidalgo
   - Ana Navarro
   - Jorge Ramos
   - Bill Richardson
   - Justice Sonia Sotomayor

3. The women's movement has had the following leaders:
   - Bella Abzug
   - Angela Davis

- Betty Friedan
- Ruth Bader Ginsburg
- Barbara Jordan
- Megan Rapinoe
- Janet Reno
- Pat Schroeder
- Eleanor Smeal
- Gloria Steinem
- Faye Wattleton

Forgotten People do not have leaders who promote the positive agendas that the aforementioned did for the groups that they represented. Where is a strong individual who grew up in Appalachia, eastern Oregon, or the panhandles of Florida, Texas, or Oklahoma who can advocate for well-being of the Forgotten People?

What Democrats consider to be logical arguments to provide a hand up (as opposed to a handout) to Forgotten People have largely fallen on deaf ears. This is well explored by Thomas Frank in his 2005 book, *What's the Matter with Kansas?* It may be that the core of the problem is Democratic policy makers have no strong leaders with whom to partner in the Forgotten American community; no one with whom to address issues and craft policy.

There is a certain irony in this lack of leadership. Four of the six post-World War II Democratic presidents were white and lived in poverty or very close to others who were poor. Those four presidents were Harry Truman, Lyndon Johnson, Jimmy Carter, and Bill Clinton. The other two Democratic presidents were John F. Kennedy and Barack Obama. But in the cases of Truman, Johnson, Carter, and Clinton, none campaigned or governed on policies designed to directly benefit the people from the areas where they grew up. These presidents were more concerned with the common good, with a global well-being. As they advanced policies to benefit most American citizens as well as others around the world, they left behind hardscrabble white people living in the communities where they grew up.

Why is it that the people who lived where they grew up became forgotten? Perhaps the reason is this group was ashamed to advocate for itself. They did not want to be another group like African Americans, Hispanics, or immigrants, who seemed to always be asking for more. They had pride, but it was a false pride.

I remember going to the Poor People's Campaign[1] in Washington, DC, in the rainy spring of 1968. It had been organized in part by Dr. Martin Luther King Jr. prior to his assassination in April of that year. The idea was to include poor people of any color, and, to an extent, it did. But most of the white people who were there were like me—not petitioning

---

1 "Wikipedia," https://en.wikipedia.org/wiki/Poor_People's_Campaign

for their own grievances but trying to help African Americans and others who were living in shanties and being pelted with relentless rain. My main contribution was to do some grocery shopping and delivery for people from my hometown of St. Louis.

When was the last time that you saw poor white people advocating for themselves? In 1932, during the Great Depression before Franklin D. Roosevelt became president, there was the Bonus Army March on Washington, DC. Most of the protestors were World War I veterans, who were white, petitioning for the bonus payments that were due to them. President Herbert Hoover ordered General Douglas MacArthur—yes, that General MacArthur—to drive the protesters away with tanks, fixed bayonets, and tear gas.

It is small wonder that if Forgotten Americans are a group with minimal pride, or false pride, that they fall victim to the demagoguery of Donald Trump or previously George Wallace. While Forgotten Americans are as old as the earliest non-Native American settlers in America, they are still in an embryonic stage of development. They lack two key ingredients of success: (a) the ability to advocate for their own well-being and (b) leadership to show them the way.

The Democratic Party has not successfully reached out to them in recent years. It is very difficult to try to help people who don't want to help themselves or accept other people's help. But that does not exonerate the Democratic Party from ignoring the group and not even having them on their radar screen except as the tools of renegade Republicans and extremist movements.

This is a tough challenge, but it will never be solved by ignoring it. And so long as the solutions lie dormant, other groups, such as African Americans, Hispanics, and immigrants, will be held hostage to the Forgotten Americans' self-pity. While they cannot successfully advocate for themselves, they can be major obstacles to the advancement of other deserving groups.

Democrats need to care, to engage, to be creative, and perhaps most important, try to empower this group in new and different ways that aren't the formula for minorities. It is a long row to hoe, but we have to start now. Let's stop the demonizing and begin the engagement.

Chapter 2
REACHING OUT TO THE FORGOTTEN PEOPLE

I REMEMBER MANY YEARS AGO taking the semi-southern route driving from St. Louis to Washington, DC. Rather than taking the shortest route on I-70 through Indianapolis and Columbus then onto the Pennsylvania Turnpike and down through Maryland, I took the Appalachian route. I had read about the poverty in eastern Kentucky and West Virginia but wanted to see it in person.

When I took this trip, I did not know I would be going through the heart of what would later become Trump Country. Leaving St. Louis, I went through southern Illinois, sometimes called Little Dixie. Democrats win Illinois by piling up huge majorities in Chicago and its suburbs, but the further south that you go in the state, the redder it gets. Like Kentucky and West Virginia, there is coal mining in southern Illinois, but its high sulfur content makes it less valuable than coal from farther east.

Central Kentucky is beautiful farmland and very white. The eastern party of Kentucky is truly coal country, where there is rugged individualism coupled with extreme poverty. Towns like Harlan, Hazard, and Pikesville were fascinating to visit, and the people were truly hardscrabble. They were also almost exclusively white. The same was true of West Virginia. The final leg was through Virginia, which had been part of the Confederacy in the Civil War.

These are areas that voted solidly Democratic during FDR's New Deal and Lyndon Johnson's Great Society. But when 1968 brought Richard Nixon and George Wallace, poor whites found new ways to vent their frustration through fear and even hate. That trumped the faint hope that the Democratic Party was offering at that time.

As I look back on that trip now, I can't help but think that as far as the contemporary Democratic Party is concerned, that part of America does not exist. Just listen to the voices at the Democratic convention in August 2020. You hear from virtually every group that could exist in America—African Americans, Hispanics, recent immigrants, Native Americans, LGBTQ people, others with disabilities but not the poor white people who live along that route from St. Louis to Washington. They populate most counties in each of the fifty states.

While conservatives are the primary obstacle to progressive legislation and improved quality of life in America, we progressives bear a large measure of the responsibility for why America is not moving ahead with sensitivity, compassion, and competence.

Progressives are constantly involved in a tag game of identity politics. Each group that is part of the fabric of the Democratic Party thinks it is getting shortchanged, and now is the time for it to get its deserved special considerations.

The identity groups are many and varied, but they do not include plain old white people who are poor and struggling. Some of them are hardworking; some of them slack on the job; many of them don't have jobs.

There are numerous nonethnic identity groups in the United States. Thirty years ago, very few people talked about their sexual identity. When the closet door first opened, many brave individuals who had been fearful of acknowledging their sexual identity gradually allowed it to be known to others. Others were forced to reveal their sexuality because they were blackmailed or otherwise forced to share what had been their secret. What began as a "one-at-a-time" movement characterized by hesitancy became more of a flood, particularly when the AIDS epidemic began in 1981. Interestingly enough, major expansion of LBGTQ rights occurred during the time of the conservative John Roberts Supreme Court. And when the administration of Barack Obama lent its support, the initiative came from then Vice President Joe Biden.

But let's consider what identity politics really means. Through a clear lens, it is the path by which overlooked groups make cases for their inclusion in the American Dream and the American body politic.

Identity politics becomes negative when one of two things happen: (a) fighting among the individual groups to see whose agenda gets top priority becomes so intense that no one gets what they want, and (b) there is a group with its own identity issues excluded from the rubric within the Democratic Party.

This is where the Democratic Party seems to have a huge blind spot. The group that is missing goes by many names: the Trump Base, the Silent Majority, the "Basket of Deplorables," the "Great Unwashed," the Forgotten Americans. Some of these are misnomers because they imply the group consists entirely of economically poor and poorly educated white people. The standard thinking is the only white people who would support Donald Trump and other extremists on the right are poor white people. But this is not so. There are millions of well-educated white people who, for one reason or another, feel comfortable with Donald Trump—or fifty years ago, with George Wallace and Richard Nixon.

Racism and hate directed toward the progressive movement comes from a wide variety of sources. The Democratic Party has never been successful in attracting voters who seemingly are driven by hate. However, some of these people might see hope if it were offered to them.

What the Democratic Party has been skilled at is providing workable policy solutions to economically distressed people of all ethnicities.

Think about the Great Depression. Who are the people you see in the black-and-white or sepia photos of the period? They are people who were in bread lines; farmers who lived in the Plains and literally saw their land blown away; down-and-out people who had accumulated fortunes on Wall Street prior to the October 28, 1929, stock market crash and who a few days later walked around penniless and in a daze. What did they all have in common—or at least, most of them? They were white. This is not to say the only people who were poor were white; it is to say those who were most visible to others through the medium of photography and film were white.

What united these people in economic peril? It was their commitment to put an end to the Republican callousness and indifference of Warren G. Harding, Calvin Coolidge, and the then current president, Herbert Hoover—to try something new and dynamic with just-elected Franklin D. Roosevelt.

Thus began the New Deal. This was a deal that was going to improve the lives of all Americans, most particularly those who were truly suffering economically.

While the New Deal may have been the greatest economic boost Americans have experienced, it had major holes in it. It was pre-identity politics. Women were only incidentally included in the New Deal, generally as the wives of working men. African Americans were left to pick up the crumbs, those jobs that poor white people wouldn't take. Hispanics suffered similarly, primarily in Florida, Texas, New Mexico,

Arizona, and California. Asian Americans were overlooked until war broke out with Japan in December 1941; two months later, many were forced to live in internment camps concentrated in California but stretching as far east as eastern Arkansas along the banks of the Mississippi River.

Since the 1930s, there has been a dramatic turn in the constituencies of the Democratic Party. The blue-collar working-class white men who were the target of so much of FDR's New Deal stimulus are in reality the doughnut hole in the current base of the party. It seems that everyone with an identity that is not blue-collar and white has a niche in the Democratic Party except those who were the core of FDR's New Deal beneficiaries.

Women, who were enfranchised to vote only one hundred years ago, are a central core to the party. Their concerns, be it with voting, reproductive choice, pay equity, childcare, etc., are all front and center in the Democratic Party. Young white people, particularly those with college degrees, are also key to Democrats. We know that younger people are more liberal than older people, and educated people are more so than those with less schooling, so it is essential that Democrats diligently work to get out the vote with the young and the credentialed.[2]

---

2 "Trends in Party Affiliation Among Demographic Groups," Pew Research Center, U.S. Politics & Policy, March 20, 2018, https://www.pewresearch.org/politics/2018/03/20/1-trends-in-party-affiliation-among-demographic-groups/.

As Thomas Frank, author of *What's the Matter with Kansas*, points out, the new dominant core of the Democratic Party is professional workers. Most of these people are white, well-educated, and upwardly mobile. They are teachers, doctors, engineers, attorneys, architects, top-level administrators, investors, and more. Their interests are often at odds with white blue-collar workers. In essence, these professionals have stolen the core of the Democratic Party from FDR's working-class base.

This professional class wants to have its interests protected like any other group in our society. Professionals want their achievements honored and preserved. They are a class of credentials, and their certificates separate them from others. All the years they spent in school—perhaps studying, perhaps partying with too much booze, more likely a combination of the two—must be honored. They have their own club, or rather series of clubs. It is important that those who have not achieved what they have, those without status credentials, be kept out of the professionals' clubs. If a group's identity can be defined by who is *not* a part of the group, then professionals are those among us who are certified to be employed in a small assortment of occupations.

The idea that the election of Barack Obama and his presidency moved America into a post-racial era was quickly proven untrue. As president, Obama felt the agony of being largely helpless to deal with the indignities heaped upon African Americans such as Trayvon Martin, Michael Brown, Freddie Gray, Eric Garner, and others. Perhaps the worst disappointment he suffered was the selection of Donald Trump as president (we choose to not use the word "election" since Trump lost the popular vote by nearly three million votes and became president only because of the archaic electoral college.).

So today's Democratic Party is focused on protecting the interests of the professional class and finding secure homes for the myriad of identity groups that want "in": racial minorities, LGBTQ individuals, recent immigrants, people with disabilities, and more.

Advocating for the interests of each of these groups strengthens the party and makes it much more of a pluralistic party than the Republican Party. Even if the Republicans wanted to appeal to these groups (as the Republican National Committee recommended following Mitt Romney's loss to Obama in 2012), it would start far behind because the Democrats have such well-developed relations with each of these groups. The future looks even bleaker for the GOP with the expectation that by 2045, white people will lose their status as a majority race in the US and become just another minority.

With the Democratic Party being so well connected to active minorities in the US, why is it that Democrats lost the presidency in 2016—and almost the election? There are several reasons. Correcting these oversights is essential to Democrats winning in 2020 and also putting together a strong political alliance that can position the party to control all three branches of government for an extended period of time to enact the progressive policies that are so essential to the betterment of the nation. The Democrats need to:

1. Vastly ramp up turnout from its core groups. When Barack Obama first ran in 2008, he received record high voter turnout from African Americans, young people, and women. Those numbers fell off in his 2012 reelection and then dropped far further in 2016 when Hillary Clinton ran against Trump. Democrats need to increase turnout, and, in 2020, this seems be happening. The primary reasons are: (a) the fierce urgency of *now* (not allowing America to fall victim to a second term for Trump) and (b) the presence of Kamala Harris on the ticket, who should play a key role in dramatically increasing the turnout of the Democrats' most reliable group, African American women.
2. Stop discounting the Walmart crowd. In other words, consider attracting the votes of poor working class (and nonworking) white people whose concerns and votes are as important as any other minority group.

Why should Democrats make a concerted effort to attract the group that Hillary Clinton formerly called the "basket of deplorables?"

a. When Franklin D. Roosevelt ran in 1932 and then assumed the presidency, the reform he initiated in the country was to have the federal government become a change agent for the people, a force that would advance economic and social equity. That is still a fundamental tenet of the philosophy of the Democratic Party. However, ever since George Wallace and Richard Nixon initiated a special appeal to "the silent majority" in 1968, which in essence seized southern states from the Democratic tent, Democrats have paid minimal attention to working class whites. Wallace did not just appeal to white voters in the South. Four years later, his appeal in the North was strong enough for him to win the Michigan Democratic primary.

While Wallace did indeed talk about more economic fairness, he was only talking about white people, primarily men. His message was clearly racist, and, for many white blue-collar workers, the racism trumped any call for economic fairness.

The upshot is that for the past fifty-plus years, the Democratic Party has only casually concerned itself with Franklin D. Roosevelt's core voters. Once Wallace and Nixon demonstrated that so-called social issues could attract the descendants of FDR's main constituency to parties other than the Democratic one, Democratic strategists have not cast a wide enough net to include poor blue-collar workers.

It seems that once again in the 2020 presidential race, the Democratic Party is almost exclusively committed to its non-blue-collar constituencies. However, it would still be worthwhile for Democrats to begin trying out better strategies to appeal to the Trump base. Their ace in the hole is Joe Biden, who, like Truman, Johnson, Carter, and Clinton before him, has roots in the old base of the New Deal.

b. In the long run, Democrats need to appeal to what is now the Trump base. Failure to have done so in the past is why we did the unthinkable: shock ourselves by moving from a Barack Obama presidency to a Donald Trump presidency. We are better than this, and we have to prevent this from happening in the future. It is not an easy task because Republicans are fifty years ahead of Democrats in culling this group. We have to crack the nut of why so many Trump supporters prioritize social issues over economic ones. As we will describe later, this preference of Trump voters dramatically impacts other people, including racial minorities, in very negative ways. By choosing to not prioritize improving their own economic conditions, Trumpers make it exceedingly difficult for others to climb the economic ladder. This is why so many states have resisted accepting Medicaid expansion—because it would help minorities, people Trumpsters often do not like. As odd as it seems, many poor whites, particularly in rural areas, are willing to sacrifice their own economic gain in order to keep minorities down. This dates back to the early days of this country when non-land-owning whites in the South, who could not economically benefit from slavery because they were too poor to own them, still supported slavery because it ensured there would be a group stationed at a lower status than them.

Even though white Americans will be a minority by 2045, until then, they will still be the largest minority in the country. And 25 to 30 percent of those white people will be today's Forgotten Americans or their descendants. Even when Democrats win elections, they will be susceptible to the kind of wild swings that happened in 2016.

There are two ways to prevent or reduce this: (a) expand participation of other minority groups [something that Democrats are currently doing] and (b) find ways to connect with Forgotten Americans.

How do we do this? It's difficult, but let's look at some strategies that are well worth considering and trying.

Some of the first ideas that come to mind are frankly unlikely to work. The reason I say the ideas are losers is because I have seen them tried and they did not work, or I have suggested them in conversations and been convinced with good reason they won't work.

The first questionable idea is to assert to Forgotten Americans that they are damaging themselves by opposing government measures that would help them economically. Why this does not work is a very difficult argument for progressives to get; I continue to struggle with it. But, to many of the Forgotten People, receiving something from the government is equivalent to receiving a handout. This makes them "charity cases," and that's not who they want to be.

1. Why do many people object to receiving government handouts when they already receive them? While it

may be difficult to believe, there are people who do not acknowledge that Social Security and Medicare benefits come from the government. They have a bit of reason behind this, because in those periods of their lives when they were working and were on a payroll, they had Social Security and Medicare deductions taken from their paychecks. The line of thinking goes that upon receiving these benefits, they are only accepting what was rightfully theirs and was taken away by the government when their private employer was paying them their justified salary or wages.

The spirit of what they say is correct, but they are technically wrong. The withholdings from their checks are not stashed away with their names on it, only to be returned to them when they retire. What is withheld from their checks when they are working is used to pay the benefits to those older than them, those who have retired. When yesterday's workers are old enough to retire, they will not be getting "their money" back. Instead, they will receive what in essence is a transfer payment from people younger than they are who are currently working and have payroll deductions from their paychecks providing the money that is necessary to keep the system going.

Notice that the thrust of the argument that "I deserve the Social Security and Medicare I receive" is all about "me." It is a sense of entitlement, which is fine up to a point. But when the entitlement applies only to oneself and perhaps other people in one's family or social group, then there is a refusal to acknowledge the common good. This is outright selfish behavior, and it is real and present in our society. So, if you want to convince fellow citizens that if they are willing to accept change, they have to give up being selfish—well, that won't easily happen.

Additionally, a key part of the equation is that Social Security and Medicare are, and are seen as, programs for the middle class. For the Forgotten People, this is all fair and just. They see themselves as middle class. One of the oddities of the Forgotten People is that even those who are poor see themselves as middle class. Those living in poverty do not want to be seen as poor, because that's something that describes other people. In their minds, it is what describes African Americans and other minorities, regardless of how the percentage of minorities who have lifted themselves into the middle class has grown dramatically in recent years.

Programs like Medicaid, SNAP (Supplemental Nutrition Assistance Program), WIC (Women Infants & Children), and TANF (Temporary Assistance for Needy Families) are all seen by the Forgotten People as being for someone else. Those others are people of color. That perception does not mean Forgotten People will not avail themselves of these programs when they feel they need them. It simply means that, in the minds of Forgotten People, if they receive benefits from any of these programs, it is because society is failing them and they need it—but when minorities do, it's because they're lazy and welfare cheats.

2. While people are selfish, some resist government handouts. How can that be? Primarily because they feel that it is inappropriate, or dishonest, to take something that is not theirs, at least if it comes from the government. What so many people do not understand is that one of the key roles of the federal government is to be an agent of income redistribution. If we value the common good, then something is wrong when there are people who do not have sufficient money to live on while others have far more than is necessary.

Insensitivity to the common good is why so many of the Forgotten People live in a world that is quite different from most progressives. But what is the common good? It's a tough question.

a. In philosophy, economics, and political science, the common good refers to either what is shared and beneficial for all or most members of a given community, or alternatively, what is achieved by citizenship, collective action, and active participation in the realm of politics and public service[3]. In somewhat simpler terms, it is caring about everyone in a society and taking steps to make sure everyone gets a fair deal.

But this idea does not resonate for someone who thinks and feels there are other people in the society who are just looking for a handout or who are seeking to have their status elevated above what it naturally should be. In many cases, the thinking of Forgotten People is that when the federal government provides for those in need, it is part of an unnatural, unconstitutional, and unholy scheme to lift lesser people in our society above them. This does not mean Forgotten People will not fully cheer for the African American quarterback on the University of Alabama football

---

3 "Wikipedia," https://en.wikipedia.org/wiki/Common_good

team or for LeBron James. It simply means the Forgotten People feel there should never be in a position where there is not a group living at a level below them.
3. If many people perceive receiving something of value from the government as indicating they are a "charity case," then why are so many of the Forgotten People willing to accept charity? The primary answer is charity does not come from the government. We must keep in mind the government is the entity that tries to stick its fingers into everything. It tries to be a social equalizer when nobody asked them to do that. It is a social engineer, infringing on the individual rights of citizens, particularly those rugged ones who fend for themselves and certainly do not want interference from the government, the representative of the liberal elites who frequently send vibes that they despise the Forgotten People.

But charity is different. It comes from the kindness of the hearts of Americans. It is often religion driven, and thus it represents God's will. It is a temporary fix to help people who are in a temporary state of being down-and-out. It is given to people who would do the same thing for others when they are back on their feet.

This is not to discount charity, because without it there would be hundreds of thousands, perhaps millions, of people who would go to bed hungry or not have a roof over their heads. Many would suffer to the point they could no longer survive.

But charity has very clear limitations to its effectiveness. While $410 billion was given to charities in 2017, most of it goes to religious organizations and educational institutions. Approximately $77 billion goes to human services and organizations like the United Way. This is a pittance compared to the $2.5 trillion in transfer payments from the federal government alone to individuals. So, while the Forgotten People can willingly accept charity and praise its presence, the bottom line is that charities do not have the wherewithal to provide anything near the resources for those most in need.[4]

The reluctance of Forgotten People to support government programs that provide health care, housing, education, and direct transfer payments means that many of them continue to suffer

---

4 "Giving Statistics," Charity Navigator, accessed September 1, 2020, https://www.charitynavigator.org/index.cfm?bay=content.view&cpid=42.

economically. They do get psychological benefits from their locked-in positions of these issues. The benefits are not economic but rather a reinforcement of their view of how various social groups in America should be stratified. When poor white people do not get expanded Medicaid—or better yet, Medicare for All—neither do minorities. This allows the Forgotten People to continue to believe minorities are always asking for handouts and they (the Trump base) are clearly better people than the minorities because they do not ask the government for assistance.

There was a time when Democrats felt if they would offer programs to poor white people to help them economically, the Forgotten People would be most appreciative and gladly accept the offers. Democrats, who tend to think logically, particularly about economic issues, thought they had the answers to bringing the Forgotten People back into the fold.

What they did not understand was that many of the Forgotten People think they are better than "those other people." They would rather have higher status on some artificial scale than higher income. As Barack Obama said when he thought he was in private company, they would rather cling to their god and guns. Those are tight grasps.

Democrats should not be faulted for not understanding this; it is a difficult concept to grasp. But the bottom line is that for the Democratic Party to simply offer economic stimuli to the Forgotten People will not bring them into the Democratic camp. So the question is, how can Democrats appeal to the Forgotten People when the seemingly best strategy of offering economic gain does not work?

A partial answer, at least, can come from winding the clock back nearly ninety years to the New Deal. FDR and the Democratic Congress developed successful ways for many white people who were suffering economically to accept the government assistance they were fashioning. Here are a couple of reasons why it seemed to work then and hopefully could be fashioned for today:

1. At that point, it seemed everyone was poor. By the time FDR took office in March 1933, it had been three and a half years since the Great Depression set in. What mass media existed at that time was not portraying pictures of minorities in distress. Films showed the bread lines and the unemployment lines of primarily white people who had been working and now could not find gainful employment. So, when the New Deal programs were presented to the people, the assumption, and the appearance, was that these programs were distinctively for white people. If the programs did not benefit racial minorities, then white people did not need to worry that the government

programs would put "those other people" a leg ahead of them.

2. One of the beauties of many of the New Deal programs was they were not direct handouts; they were employment programs. Among the first programs to be passed was the Civilian Conservation Corps (CCC), which passed in 1933 and immediately hired unemployed people to work on public land projects, including upgrading national parks and building infrastructure. The same year, the Tennessee Valley Authority (TVA) was passed, and it put thousands to work containing flooding in Appalachia and developing hydroelectricity for the region. Other programs such as the Public Works Administration (PWA) and Works Progress Administration (WPA) were enacted to provide additional opportunities for people who were without jobs.

The New Deal included other direct transfer payments such as the creation of Social Security in 1935, which provided necessary income for post-retirement citizens. But because this program was designed for a special class of people to whom most of the "Forgotten People" could relate without prejudice, it was acceptable. It also promised well-earned future benefits for those "Forgotten People" who were now working.

One of the keys to the success of the New Deal was that there were opportunities for people to enter into "something-for-something" contractual arrangements. Citizens gave sweat equity in return for paychecks. In many ways, that is missing in some of today's government programs to help the poor. At a time when so much work needs to be done in the areas of infrastructure, health care, education, and environmental protection, the federal government is not initiating programs to hire people to construct and staff these projects.

To use a fashionable term, it seems Forgotten People, like most other people, are comfortable with arrangements that are *quid pro quo*. They are willing to accept something if it means they have to give something tangible in return. The simpler the better. Work for pay.

There are programs designed to help Forgotten People, and indeed they do economically help. They were generally created because the Democratic Party was looking out for them. But for reasons that are often difficult to fathom, Forgotten People may accept the largess but not embrace the program or the people who brought the programs to them.

A good example is farm subsidies. Since the New Deal, the federal government has made cash payments to farmers in return for the farmers not growing crops on certain fields. The idea is to ensure there are not unworkable surpluses of crops. By limiting supply, they are able to keep prices for farmers higher. This yields twin benefits for farmers: (a) they receive direct cash payments to make the program work and (b) they are guaranteed the prices of their crops will be high enough to make their planting and producing worthwhile. While farmers benefit from these programs, there seems to be a certain element of resentment because the government is meddling with their rights to farm how they wish.

Similarly, federal guarantees for small business loans are often unappreciated. While these loans help many entrepreneurs create or maintain small businesses that are so vital to the health of the nation and its job creators, the loans are often resented because of the paperwork involved and the fact that they represent intrusion of the federal government into free enterprise.

A primary lesson we can learn from the New Deal is people who are poor seem to accept assistance when it resembles the employment program it actually is. The idea of getting up in the morning, going to work, returning home in the evening, and receiving regular paychecks seems to be acceptable to members of the Forgotten People. They don't have to summarily reject anything because it may help minorities or other people they resent in one way or another.

Because Democrats operate much more on the basis of reason than Republicans and some independents, programs such as Medicare for All, full protection of reproductive rights, and collaboration where possible with foreign nations are central tenets to the Democratic Party. If we are going to have successful change for this country, if this change is going to be progressive, we need to do three things:

1. Clearly focus on the issues that are absolutely necessary for the country to move in a progressive direction.
2. Find ways to connect with Forgotten Americans, not just in the short run but in the long run.
3. Have proper checks and balances on the new core constituency of the Democratic Party—professionals who often separate themselves from other Americans, hiding behind their credentials and certification.

Part one is easiest. There are issues on the progressive agenda that are pretty much slam dunks. I'll spare you long explanations because they fall within the section of the Declaration of Independence that states, "We hold these truths to be self-evident, that all men are created equal, that they are endowed by their Creator with inalienable rights, and that among these are life, liberty and the pursuit of happiness."

We need to update this a bit, recognizing that at the time of the Declaration, "all men" meant all white men owning property. In today's world, this means everyone. And regarding "their Creator," we need to respect the views of our friends at the Freedom From Religion Foundation[5]

---

5 "Freedom From Religion Foundation," https://ffrf.org/

and include the caveat that some people may not believe in a Creator with a capital C.

But here are some of the issues that would seem to be central to a progressive agenda. By progressive agenda, I mean one that is based on empathy and critical thinking.

1. In the United States, and in the world, we need to eradicate the scourge of poverty. Over the past fifty years, we have made remarkable progress both domestically and globally. However, poverty cannot be dissociated from "rising expectation." In other words, poor people may now have air conditioning, internet access, smartphones, refrigerators, and food to eat most of the time, but they are frustrated when they look at others in their community who have much more wealth. According to the Economic Policy Institute[6], the average CEO in the United States is paid 271 times the salary of the typical American worker. Solving the problem of poverty requires two steps:
   a. Raising the income and wealth of poor people.
   b. Ensuring the income disparity between the poorest and the wealthiest is not so wide that poor people are frequently frustrated, feeling they do not have enough.

---

[6] "Economic Policy Institute," https://www.epi.org/

2. Health care for all. It must be affordable, comprehensive, and accessible. This should be in inner cities, rural areas, everywhere in the United States. It's called Medicare for All. Health care workers, the people who do the heavy lifting to provide for patients, must be well paid. On the other hand, insurance companies, and the money that goes to them, must be eliminated. Ample money should go into research and implementation of new health care techniques, with particular emphasis on preventative health care policies.
3. Climate change. This concept is as simple as when a child in kindergarten is told to clean up their mess. If we don't mess up, we care for the environment. This includes using energy and chemical sources that do not leave invisible messes such as too much CO_2 in the air. We need to follow scientists, not skeptics.
4. Pro-choice on reproductive rights. No one denies it can be very difficult for a woman to end the development of a fetus. But the mother is different from the fetus; she is much more in tune with the world in which we live, the challenges that she faces, and the implications of choosing to terminate a pregnancy or to carry the child to term. Not only should abortion be legal and safe, it must be accessible. It must be part of mainstream medicine, as available as an endoscopy

or an X-ray might be to a woman who wants it. If ever there were an issue where the government should not get involved, it is reproductive choice.

5. Upgrade and expand our infrastructure. This has been largely ignored for decades. Other countries have much better roads, bridges, tunnels, airports, train service, and multimodal systems than the United States. The US seemed to stop when the country came to believe government spending was wasteful. We must recognize the obvious: no one else is going to build the roads or the airports. The beauty of infrastructure development is that it provides us with needed societal improvements, it creates millions of jobs in a variety of occupations, and we can do it in a way that is environmentally sound, further enhancing our quality of life. Perhaps most important, developing infrastructure provides meaningful and well-paying jobs to Forgotten People in ways that are seen as fair contracts and not handouts or government manipulation.

Chapter 3
CONNECTING SCHOOLS TO THE COMMON GOOD

IMPROVE OUR SCHOOLS. THIS may be the most difficult of all of our core challenges. Traditional thinking, even by progressives, is that better schools are characterized by (a) the amount of money spent on them, (b) better test scores, (c) better facilities, (d) better sports teams, and (e) generally more things to brag about.

While each of these components other than (d) and (e) play key roles in improving schools, they do not include the key component. Most importantly, schools must be designed to best serve the needs of each individual student, and every one of them is different. Teaching must be empathetic and involve critical, compassionate thinking. Our goal should be for students to develop into the best people they can be, not robots about whom school districts, administrators, and parents can brag.

Over the last half century, one of the fastest-growing sectors in our economy has been educational bureaucracies. It used to be that schools were largely autonomous, even public schools. But as schools wanted to better advocate for themselves, they developed hierarchical organizations like virtually every other profession. Years ago, a public school district would have a superintendent and several assistants, perhaps ones for building and grounds, one for purchasing, one for finance. Most teachers graduated from college with degrees in something other than education, and they brought the knowledge they gained from the subject in which they had majored into the classroom. But education departments at universities ballooned and, along with them, the school bureaucracies and the state departments of education.

What transpired in schools on a day-to-day basis became much more of a top-down and prescribed approach.

Education, like most professions, tends to see the world through its own lens. It does not see itself as an agent of social change, of helping to raise new generations of citizens who are empathetic and committed to advancing the well-being of all.

This is an area where I tend to side with some conservatives, at least those who advocate for free enterprise played on a level playing field. I would like to see schools operate in an open market, with choice for parents and students. I would like to see a premium on innovation. I'd like for schools to be genuine communities where everyone can be engaged in promoting the well-being of everyone else, as well as the societal common good.

In some ways, schools are very complicated; in other ways, they are simple. Right now, for the benefit of our greater society, and also the specific interests of the Democratic Party, we need schools to "lighten up," to throw off the yoke of top-down mandates and become communities where learning is fun and purposeful. We must keep in mind that it is difficult for adults to learn about and value the common good if it not a concept that is discussed and valued when in school.

Obsession with test scores and grades isolate school administrators and teachers from creating classrooms in which students develop as healthy individuals and contributing members of the society in which they live.

School reform is difficult, but it must be in the direction of further empowering students and their commitment to a greater good. We may be turning the corner now, but school change still remains one of the greatest necessities to making our political system more democratic, functional, and compassionate.

Chapter 4

DEMOCRATIZING HOW GOVERNMENT WORKS

Over the long run, we need to fix the structural inequities within our government. Each of the items listed below is an obstacle to democracy and thus has disproportionate impact on minorities, women, the Forgotten People, and others who do not have clear access to political power. Among the steps we need to take to eliminate the most egregious barriers to true democracy are:

1. **Abolish and replace the electoral college.** Five times in the history of the United States, the winner of the presidential election has not finished with the most popular votes. It has already happened twice in this century, and the result has been two of the worst presidents we have had (George W. Bush and Donald Trump). I know there is a revisionist theory that W was okay. True, he was, and apparently is, a nice guy. But he took America into two needless wars that we are still fighting, and he destroyed the balanced

budgets of the Bill Clinton era with needless tax cuts for the wealthy.

If you are unclear as to why the electoral college is unfair, just consider the following scenario. Suppose that Candidate A wins Wyoming by 100,000 votes. By winning Wyoming, she would receive three electoral votes. Now, suppose that Candidate B wins California but by half the margin, 50,000 votes. He would receive 55 electoral votes. At this point, Candidate B, who carried California, would be winning the electoral vote in a landslide, 55 to 3. But Candidate A would have more popular votes because she carried Wyoming by a larger margin than he carried California. With two states "reporting," Candidate A should be leading because she has more popular votes, but instead it would be Candidate B with the electoral majority.

The damage done by the electoral college is insidious. Most states tend to go red (Republican) or blue (Democrat). In many ways, voters in these noncompetitive states are disenfranchised because their votes really don't count; the state is going to go the way it's going to go due to the electoral college.

There are arguably twelve states that are in play, are purple, are competitive, and are swing states. According to 538[7], they are Colorado, Florida, Iowa, Michigan, Minnesota, Nevada, New Hampshire, North Carolina, Ohio, Pennsylvania, Virginia, and Wisconsin. If you live in any one of these dozen states, you will get lots of visits from presidential candidates (in "normal" times), see far more commercials from the candidates, and generally have more money spent in your state on behalf of the candidates. If you live in the other 38 states, including our three of the four largest, California, Texas, and New York, you're S.O.L.

There are alternatives to the electoral college, like the National Public Vote Interstate Compact, but it would be unreliable and not locked in with constitutional authority.[8] The only true way to have a democracy in how America elects its president and vice president is to have a constitutional amendment that eliminates the electoral college and replaces it with the popular vote, giving equal weight to all people.

---

7 "FiveThirtyEight," https://fivethirtyeight.com
8 "National Popular Vote Interstate Compact," Wikipedia, accessed September 1, 2020, https://en.wikipedia.org/wiki/National_Popular_Vote_Interstate_Compact

2. **Eliminate or minimize gerrymandering.** What is gerrymandering? This is best explained by the words that former Supreme Court Justice Potter Stewart used when he was asked to describe pornography: "I know it when I see it." Just for fun, it's good to read his entire statement: "I shall not today attempt further to define the kinds of material I understand to be embraced within that shorthand description ["hard-core pornography"], and perhaps I could never succeed in intelligibly doing so. But I know it when I see it, and the motion picture involved in this case is not that."

Gerrymandering involves drawing legislative districts in ways that favor one party over the other. For example, in Missouri, six of the eight congressional seats are held by Republicans, and they have been so since redistricting in 2010. Both of the Democratic districts in Missouri are "minority majority" ones, meaning the population is majority African American and so are the representatives. But in the presidential election of 2008, right before the redistricting, Barack Obama lost to John McCain by less than 4,000 votes, 0.14 percent of the vote. Missouri was then a swing state. The Tea Party wave of 2010 resulted in Missouri's state legislature being overwhelmingly Republican, and they gerrymandered their districts and the congressional districts to drastically favor their party. But since 2000, Democrats have won most statewide elections, and legislative districts should be drawn to reflect that ratio.

Democrats are known to gerrymander as well. The answer to prevent it is to have computers programmed by nonpartisan individuals craft boundaries so as many districts as possible reflect the overall party distribution in the state. When this is not feasible, which happens frequently, then the proper guidelines are that the district be "compact and contiguous." Examples of districts that are not compact and contiguous but are drawn to favor one party or the other include:

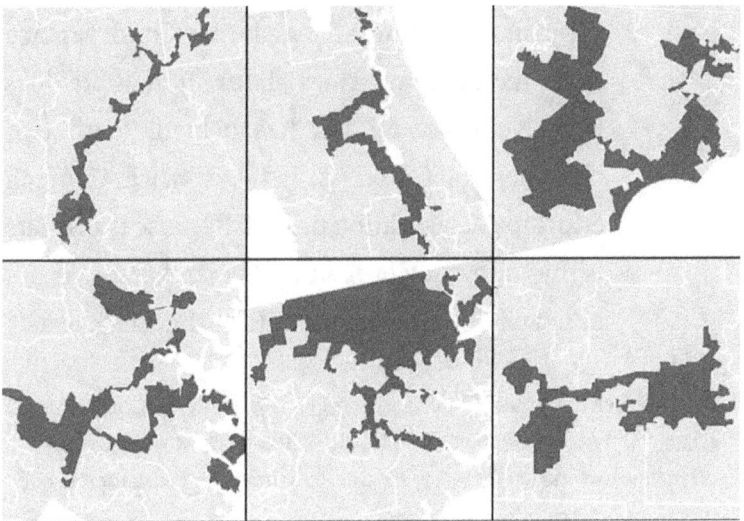

This should be eliminated. Districts must be able to pass the "giggle test."⁹

3. **Revamp the ways in which legislative bodies operate.** Our founding fathers were cautious, and, in the era of Trump, we can understand the virtue in that. But if we are going to move ahead, we need to reduce the obstacles to effective legislation. Franklin D. Roosevelt accomplished a remarkable amount but never quite got his *Economic Bill of Rights* passed. If there had been fewer obstructionists in Congress and on the Supreme Court, he may have led us much closer to the full safety net that government provides in so many other advanced economic societies. Here are some suggestions for making legislative bodies more efficient and, indeed, far more democratic.

   a. **Eliminate bicameral legislatures and replace with one unicameral legislature.** One state does this, Nebraska, and it has helped. With two chambers of Congress, it takes twice as much effort to get legislation passed. Because the Senate is the "odd body out" since its membership is not based on population, it should go. But since Senate

---

9 Christopher Ingraham, "America's Most Gerrymandered Congressional Districts," *Washington Post*, May 15, 2014, https://www.washingtonpost.com/news/wonk/wp/2014/05/15/americas-most-gerrymandered-congressional-districts/?arc404=true

representation is based on equal representation from each of the fifty individual states, that will be very difficult to do. We should keep in mind that states are essentially anachronisms, and effective governance really involves representatives at the national and local level.
b. **Dramatically decrease the powers of the leaders of Congress and committee chairs.** We need look no further than Senate Majority Leader Mitch McConnell. For ten years, he has successfully blocked needed legislation like gun control and environmental protection from coming to the floor of the Senate. Yes, he is entitled to oppose such legislation but not to keep it from being debated and voted upon. His extensive power, and the fear of his Senate Republican colleagues to challenge him, essentially make him a mini dictator. In the House of Representatives, the Speaker has similar powers, though currently Nancy Pelosi uses it much more judiciously.

For good reason, each chamber has numerous committees and subcommittees within the committees. This is so members can specialize in issues and have the resources to study possible legislation and oversight and ultimately draft legislation. Sounds good—an excellent structure to divide up responsibility among members and simplify the drafting of legislation. Unfortunately, within each committee, the chairpersons have the same power that the Senate Majority Leader or Speaker of the House has within the entire chambers. They can block the consideration of issues, the calling of witnesses, and the drafting of legislation. There are dozens of mini fiefdoms within each house of Congress.

If we as citizens of the United States believe true democracy means each of us should have equal say in the decisions that are made (one person = one vote), then that's the way that it should be in Congress. Both procedural and substantive decisions should be made by the majority, with full recognition of minority rights. This is an issue that is largely distant from the American people, but it needs to come to the fore since it has such a dramatic impact on why meaningful legislation is so difficult to pass.

The last meaningful gun control legislation was passed in 1994, and we all know of the horrendous mass shootings and violence on the streets since then. The Voting Rights Act of 1965 was found unconstitutional by the Supreme Court for dubious reasons in 2013. The court's ruling can be circumvented by meaningful legislation in Congress, but it has gone nowhere since then, with the Senate being controlled by Republicans and the House for most of that time. Voter suppression has dramatically increased since 2013. We are moving backward. Reforming the way in which Congress operates so it more properly reflects majority views of the American public is essential for us to have needed legislation and for citizens to feel more confident in the way our government operates.

c. **Reducing or eliminating the role of money in politics.** If there is anything that undermines the concept of equality among voters, it is the private funding of campaigns. We need to move to public financing so each candidate has ample resources to run an effective campaign and no one candidate has far more resources than another. Here are a few reasons why our current system undermines democracy:

1. Huge amounts of money are given to candidates or to committees working for their election. Much of the time, the donors

are hidden by laws that do not require their names to be public.

2. Candidates who know people with "deep pockets" can raise far more money than other candidates. This is clearly not fair.
3. Decent candidates spend six hours a day or more "dialing for dollars." There is no way to avoid the reality that this makes candidates beholden to donors. It also means candidates are spending time with the rich and wealthy and therefore avoiding necessary contact with the majority of constituents in their districts—the people who have the problems government needs to address.

Candidates take on different personalities when they become consumed with fundraising. They begin to talk the language of the very rich, they spend time socializing with the very wealthy, and they gradually lose touch with the constituents who most need their help.

d. **Reform our presidential primary system.** Kamala Harris is the Democratic vice presidential nominee, but, in her run for president in 2020, she did not even make it as far as the first competition for the primary, the Iowa caucuses in early

February. Lots of good candidates dropped out before Iowa. Why did she?
1. Her fate was determined by polls, not actual voting.
2. Money. Her donor base was drying up.
3. Her prospects did not look good in Iowa.

If the first primary had been in her home state of California, she would have polled well and performed well in the primary. But that's not the way the rules are written. The first two competitions are in Iowa and New Hampshire, both well over 90 percent white and largely rural. Next is Nevada, which is not a primary, and many voters cannot participate. Then comes South Carolina, in which the Democratic voters are heavily weighted to African American. That's fine, except it's not a true reflection of America.

We need to move away from scattershot primaries and have regional ones that reflect a broader base of the American population. With public financing, all candidates could compete if they met a certain threshold in the polls. The outcome of the voting would be better if we used Ranked Choice Voting[10].

---

10 "Wikipedia, Ranked voting" https://en.wikipedia.org/wiki/Ranked_voting

Democrats are fortunate to have such a fine candidate as Joe Biden representing them in 2020. But the system is fraught with pitfalls. Democrats talk about democracy. Now is the time to make the primary system much fairer, giving more equal representation to all voters.

If we are going to have a country in which there is a clear and consistent majority favoring progressive policies, we have to do more than employ political strategies. The eight years stretching from 2008 to 2016 vividly reveal how far the American political pendulum can swing. We have far too many people who have not thought through their political views to make them real convictions, so they can whimsically jump on a Barack Obama bandwagon one year and be on the Donald Trump one the next year.

Without firm beliefs, they easily swing from side to side as American popular culture changes.

As we have mentioned, an essential component of a healthy body politic is having a committed concern for the common good. The common good refers to what is shared and beneficial for all or most members of a given community. All societies, including the United States, have countervailing forces at work when it comes to promoting the common good. Many people value promoting what is best for society as a whole, but this view often runs in conflict with the protection of individual liberties.

Some individual liberties work compatibly with promoting the common good. Freedom of speech, of assembly, and of the press protect the rights of individuals who want to exercise these constitutional rights, but they also can be means of promoting the common good. Other rights, such as the Second Amendment, seem to place a disproportionate amount of power in the hands of the person who is exercising this right, at the expense of promoting the common good. In other words, an individual may consider his or her right to bear arms as inviolate. If this right trumps all other considerations, then it undermines the advancement of the common good. The more guns there are in a society, the more likely some of them will be used in anger, or accidentally, to inflict harm on others. Currently, there are approximately 393 million firearms in the United States—a country with a population of 330 million.[11]

Most people who own these guns are not casual about this. They consider gun ownership an essential right and, in fact, a cultural indication of who they are. If anyone were to seriously suggest we confiscate guns from gun owners, they

---

11 Christopher Ingraham, "There Are More Guns Than People in the United States, According to a New Study of Global Firearm Ownership," *Washington Post*, June 19, 2018, https://www.washingtonpost.com/news/wonk/wp/2018/06/19/there-are-more-guns-than-people-in-the-united-states-according-to-a-new-study-of-global-firearm-ownership/.

would have no idea how fruitless that would be. The first steps would inevitably lead to bloodshed at the doorsteps of Americans who insist on protecting their right to own guns.

Obviously, the counterargument to making gun ownership a sacrosanct right is that each gun represents a measure of danger to the citizenry at large (i.e., the common good). The more guns in circulation, the more will be available for people to use in crimes. It may be that many gun owners are responsible, but the black market for guns is huge with so many readily available.

Indeed, there are many gun owners who are responsible and understand the concept of the common good. There are also millions of gun owners who have good reason to own a firearm, particularly those living in rural areas where there are natural threats to their safety. But there is an ugly history to the intense belief many gun owners have in the Second Amendment.

Many historians believe the main reasoning behind the Second Amendment ("A well-regulated Militia, being necessary to the security of a free State, the right of the people to keep and bear Arms, shall not be infringed.") was to ensure slaveholders would be able to easily hunt down—and, if necessary, shoot—runaway or recalcitrant slaves. Similarly, permitting white people to own guns was considered a necessity in clearing the land of Native Americans.

That mindset of "white is right" clearly carries on today. Many white gun owners consciously or subconsciously think their right to own a gun is what stands between them and their fear that minorities and other "rabble-rousers" will rebel against white rule and turn the country upside down.

Clearly, the presence of so many guns in this country—and more so, so many rabid gun owners—is a force at odds with promoting the common good. It certainly undermines the quality of life of minorities, particularly African Americans. So many of the guns slip away from their original, sometimes licensed, owners and make their way onto the streets to unlicensed owners. Shootings are rampant in many poor African American and Hispanic neighborhoods. Gunshot deaths are now the leading cause of death of young African Americans. Police shootings are the sixth leading cause of death for young black men.

One could argue that if there were not so many guns in the hands of Americans, and so many floating around in our inner cities, the police would need not be so heavily armed and so quick to use firearms against innocent victims. The gun culture in America has an ugly history, and present-day guns present numerous threats, both intended and unintended.

Whether gun owners are white "my home is my castle" proponents or inner-city gang members, their ownership of guns is a way for them to exercise their individual liberties.

It does not promote the common good or make our society safer.

Finding ways to reduce the strength of the gun culture in America is similar to finding ways for Forgotten People to become full-fledged members of the Democratic political base. It is clear they have not been impacted by mass shootings such as at Sandy Hook Elementary School in Newtown, Connecticut, or at Marjorie Stoneman Douglas High School in Parkland, Florida. The logic that is so clear to most progressives seems to be thoroughly missing among many gun owners, especially in their advocacy groups such as the National Rifle Association (NRA).

Diminishing the damage that gun owners inflict on the United States will take many years, even decades. Some of the steps we have suggested for bringing the Forgotten People into the Democratic tent, such as more jobs programs, may help in reducing the gun culture in America. But in the long run, it will take advanced measures to make empathy a key characteristic of our populace and body politic.

There are organizations working to ramp up the vote for progressives. The Voter Participation Center (VPC)[12] has a well-designed strategy of attracting infrequent voters to engage, one election at a time. They target three demographic groups: unmarried women, young people, and racial minorities. Their

---

12 Voter Participation Center website, https://www.voterparticipation.org/

research shows that when members of these groups vote, 70 percent of the time they vote for Democratic candidates.

Using direct mail, VPC showers these people with encouragement to (a) register to vote if they have not registered and (b) vote in upcoming elections. Their research shows they get increased positive responses by sending direct mailers up to six times to potential voters. You may think there would be a backlash because it's overkill, but their research indicates ongoing solicitation to register or vote brings positive results.

This is obviously an expensive endeavor, and VPC raises tens of thousands of dollars to fund these targeted mailings. But it is important to note what VPC claims: they are very effective in increasing the participation of Democratic voters in elections. What they do not claim is that they change people's minds beyond the occurrence of the next election.

Indeed, this is a very short-term approach, something that has a short half-life every election. As Barack Obama said in his remarkable speech to the 2020 Democratic convention, "Democracy was never meant to be transactional—you give me your vote; I make everything better. It requires an active and informed citizenry."[13]

---

13 "New York Times, Watch Obama's Full Speech at the Democratic National Convention" https://www.nytimes.com/2020/08/19/us/politics/obama-speech.html

So, while we can try the blanket direct mail approach of the Voter Participation Center in the short run, we are going to have to find ways for far more citizens of all identity groups to grow real connections between themselves and the common good. If we have a continuum with individual liberties on one end and the common good on the other, we need to move the slider closer to the common good point.

In order for us to make progress, or at least minimize the chances of having another "Trump regression," we need to focus on both short-term solutions and long-term ones. So here is the proposed three-pronged strategy for the progressive movement and the Democratic Party for both the short term and the long term.

1. Work to bring Forgotten Americans into your tent, giving them the same status and importance as any other identity group. Engage in affirmative action with this group, identifying young people who can become future leaders and providing them with educational and vocational opportunities that will help them develop into strong community leaders. Ensure the messaging of the Democratic Party includes Forgotten Americans along with every other group.
2. Work to reform the structure of our government so it is tilted toward action rather than inaction. This means removing barriers like the electoral

college, gerrymandering, voter suppression, and the undemocratic organization of legislative bodies, including Congress. Make the functioning of government as democratic as we want out elections to be.
3. Reform schools so the mandates of the educational bureaucracy are greatly diminished and replaced with a common-sense commitment to the holistic development of each student. Provide choice for parents and students and make school fun. Help schools have visions that move beyond the myopic view of themselves and instead always have an eye on the greater good for all.

In the short run, the good news is that we have Joe Biden at the top of the ticket in 2020. He can and will reach out to Forgotten Americans. But with changing demographics, it may be a long time until we have another Democratic nominee who comes from roots similar to Harry Truman, Lyndon Johnson, Jimmy Carter, Bill Clinton, and Joe Biden. That may be good as we have more diverse nominees. But now is an opportune time to bring the Forgotten People into the fold, a time that may not repeat itself for decades as other identity groups in the Democratic Party cycle their way through presidential nominees. Above all else, we need global vision. Here's hoping we can all rise to the challenge.

WHAT WE CAN DO NOW

WE ALL NEED TO work on our peripheral vision, seeing the entire playing field. That's what makes a great catcher in baseball, an outstanding quarterback in football, a savvy point guard in basketball, and a dominant goalie in hockey.

So many forces in our society call upon us to "narrowcast," to do the opposite of using peripheral vision. When we select a channel on TV, we are zooming in. When we identify with a particular religion, we are leaving out others. When we advocate for any subgroup of society, we leave other groups out.

To anyone reading this book prior to November 3, 2020, I would urge you to think about the common good, the greater good, that which is best for the greatest number of people. It seems like a reasonable concept, but it's incredibly difficult when we become absorbed with our own personal needs, or those of our family and friends, or those of our state or even country.

Politics can be a form of war, using a divide and conquer strategy. This is antithetical to building a healthy society. Unfortunately, dividing and conquering is also frequently a winning strategy.

What is unique about the Democratic Party is individuals within it seem to have the capacity to embrace others who are different from them. Wealthy white suburbanites can support educational policies that benefit children who have far fewer resources than their own children. Women activists are staunch supporters of Native American rights. Environmentalists protect plants and animals and integrate that with the health of human beings.

There are two things that people with progressive ideas can do now:

1. If you are a member of the Forgotten People and you want to advance the causes so essential to people like you, become a leader of the movement. Show the world thought, concern, and hope. Let others know that while those among you who live in hate and fear may be loud, they are not who you want representing you.
2. If you are a member of any of the dozens or scores of identity groups within the Democratic Party, continue to advance the causes closest to you. But view the world through peripheral lenses and do not overlook the Forgotten People. It might make all the difference in 2020—and hopefully well beyond that.

ACKNOWLEDGMENTS

Special thanks to my wife, Gloria Bilchik, with whom I have an ongoing lively conversation about the issues central to this book. She provides challenging thoughts while offering unwavering support.

Thanks also to the Civitas staff and the 2020 summer interns, as well as the outstanding guest presenters who raised so many important ideas for us to consider. My hope is that the Civitas interns continue to be idealistic, visionary, and pragmatic. I have suggested to them that it gets harder as we get older. Every generation of youth hears the future of the world is in their hands. Interns, figure out when it's real and when it's B.S.

Thanks also to my wonderful high school friends and the wonder of Zoom, which has allowed us to reconnect in meaningful ways. We basically talk about politics and sports—if there's an afterlife, we'll continue the conversation.

I have wanted to work with editor Kim Bookless for some time and was fortunate enough to be able to do so for this book. It's rare to find someone who is so knowledgeable about the rules but also flexible enough to allow common sense to prevail where desirable.

Thanks also to Michele DeFilippo and Ronda Rawlins of 1106 Design, who crafted a very handsome cover. Thanks also to freelancer Kayla Hargrove who helped with the initial concept.

Tony Chellini and Kelly Santaguida of Gatekeeper Press could not have made it easier to publish the book.

Dan Smith, Mike Onorato and Ann Kaiser of Smith Publicity were key to reaching readers with the urgency of the impending election.

www.ingramcontent.com/pod-product-compliance
Lightning Source LLC
LaVergne TN
LVHW011856060526
838200LV00054B/4366